Makings of a Man

Jalil Q Oates

DEDICATION

To my beautiful mother Latoya C.Oates. (As Zion by Lauryn Hill plays in the background). I simply take the time out to Thank you & Apologize. Thank you for never shielding me from the truths of this world, because that exposure ultimately prepped me for all of the experiences & obstacles this life would throw at me throughout my adolescents.

Thank you for my siblings, my older brothers mistakes have always been my biggest lessons. My sister's presence is a constant reminder of you, she has your attitude completely .

Thank you for never needing a man, because of that I never needed a father. I never made excuses& looked for solutions instead, he missed out not us!

I apologize if I ever made you feel like any other woman could compete with you, like any other woman could make claims to the pieces of my heart that have mom engraved in them.

I apologize because if life has taught me anything . It's that you only get one mother & I love you more than anything in this world <3…

There wasn't anything in this world that you thought I couldn't do. My biggest fan, you motivated me to make something of myself. I hope that I can take this light that shines on me and be a beacon of hope for young men growing up in similar circumstances. I don't regret anything I've experienced because in so many ways it has contributed to the man I am today. I love you mom, continue to guide me and watch over my journey.

CONTENTS

ACKNOWLEDGMENTS

To Loved Ones and Lost Ones, to Family and Friends, to Mentors and Mentee's, To Bosses and Janitors, to Success Stories and Tragic Tales, to Great and Terrible Experiences, to the Things I've Obtained, to the things I've Lost. To the Heartache and Happiness. There is not a Person, Place or Thing that I've experienced that I Regret. I'm Thankful for the Scars and what I've Learned in and Throughout the Process of Healing. All of this has made me into the Man I am Today

1 PREFACE

Being a young man from the inner city there was so much that I didn't know because of the things I was subjected to each and every day. Each day we saw the crime filled neighborhoods, where the man with the money gets the respect.

I'm from a era where we took long walks after school through drug and gang infested territory . To the buildings we resided in, where the elevators were usually out of service. An the stairways, reeked with the smell of urine. A neighbor became family, an what you saw each day was all you knew. But little did I know, there was an even bigger world outside of everything that I was exposed to.

Did you know that we've only explored roughly 5% of the ocean on the globe? All countries combined!

I say that to say this, Imagine living your entire lifetime and only knowing the 1% of the world you live in. Because that is the case for most people living in urban environments. Many people are conditioned to not aspire for things outside of their Environments.

Where I'm from it was ok to see someone hustling on the corner & to know what they were doing was wrong . But it was the way they fed their family . In most cases, the only way for them to provide for their families. The job opportunities were scarce & people as some would say "Had to get it , how they live it. "
There weren't many real success stories. I often wondered how my aunt and mother still knew the same people, living in the same neighborhoods. Since they were young . I often compare the real world to the lives of the actors on television or movies. You can honestly gain different perspectives and insights into various social classes from the lives portrayed by your favorite actors/ actress.

Watching these shows became my escape from the lower class. In the movies I would notice when someone moved into a new neighborhood they were complete strangers.

In my town, wherever you moved chances are you knew majority of the people living around you. To me at one point of my life, all of these things seemed normal. I accepted life for what it was then reevaluated things. I then painted a mental picture of how I wanted it to be someday. This became the X factor. With this image, I assessed what will help me make this image a reality and subtract what I felt didn't or would take away from my potential. In grammar school, we would have activities in which we would be asked to say what we wanted to be when we grew up. In my dreamy childhood imagination my honest answer was Hercules, and I wanted my wife to be Xenia the warrior princess. But instead I opted to say just like my favorite recreational staff member. H would give al f us a dollar every once in a blue. I saw his job as something attainable instead of wanting to be a cop, doctor , or a lawyer. I didn't think people of those professions , came from environments similar to mine.

We didn't want to play, be dreamy act adventurous . We were too busy trying to find our way.

At a young age I wasn't too good at sports, I didn't play a lot in the summer rec. basketball leagues. I only got a chance to play or see the court if my team was winning by a lot. So in my mind I thought to myself I wasn't good enough, but little didn't I know I was still young.

I was handicapped to begin with by not having a father present during these times to tell me "Hey Kid, It's just the beginning . If you work hard you'll get better."

Those positive inspirational talks didn't exist very often in my life or the other kids that resided in my community.

Too many youths my age were not able to realize that they were young and filled with potential.

If you were lucky enough to have a jump shot, and good dribble or run with a football faster than everyone else and score, you were a part of a group of very few that had a better opportunity of making it out. But if you didn't you felt like a failure. People didn't see further than sports. With so many professions out there.

" You either sling crack rock , or got a wick jump shot" - BIG

Most young men find themselves even saying "Maybe I'll just start hanging with the local cliques and figuring out ways to rob and steal. To take as opposed to earning the things needed to provide for their family.

I think my generation was the last in the era of the "Playground Kids" or the 80's babies. The era where doing stupid things were normal , getting into trouble or being a trouble maker was actually cool. But luckily for me, fast forward to present day. Mid 20's with a MBA, no kids and never been convicted of any crimes. I say 'convicted" because although I was charged and arrested with a million dollar bail. I was in the wrong place at the wrong time. All of my charges after a year of attending court were dropped and my record expunged. The happy ending most of my peers never have seen. An experience that I don't promote in any way. If I could've avoided I would. After all I've seen and been through who would've thought I'd be here, where I am today!

Life didn't drastically change for me. I was still brought up in the same neighborhoods . Only thing that set me apart was what I knew and did with that information. By being exposed to different things. It can change a person's mindset. If you have nothing & all you see if nothing, that is all you will ever want. But if your exposed to everything in the right way, it will become apparent that you are more than capable of going to the places and acquiring the things that make you happy. It's not about being the greatest success. It's all about living the happiest life that you know you are in control of. The feeling of control : over our lives ,our decisions. What we want to eat, what we want to wear. All comes from taking accountability of ourselves and the decisions we make in life, with money, relationship, careers etc. With that comes the control, and that control breeds happiness.

Stop!
Before you continue reading, Draw a picture of how you want your life to be and how you see yourself in ten years from now. I hope that after this book you acknowledge that you are capable of making this an reality for yourself. Impossible is I'm possible!

"I AM NO BIRD AND NO NET ESNARES ME: I AM A FREE HUMAN BEING WITH AN INDEPENDENT WILL".

- CHARLOTTE BRANTE

2 CHARACTER

Character – *The mental and Moral qualities "distinctive" to an individual.*
    Distinctive – *Characteristics of a person or thing and so serving to distinguish it from others.*

Take a look at yourself & what sets you apart from the rest. If I had to tell you my most important characteristics. Most likely mine will be different from yours. **What I value, cherish and work for will be different because we are individuals**. You are the main character in your life. Too often I see individuals living a life as supporting cast to someone else's livelihood or well-being. I'd admit, I even fell into the trap myself. But I challenge you to look deep into yourself. To value yourself, your goals and most importantly everything you want out of life, an what you want to accomplish.

I value amongst other things my sincerity and trustworthiness. I want people to trust me , because I want to be able to trust others. Looking pass the façade of what people want you to see. I'm able to draw genuine connections in an attempt to surround myself with positive energy & people. Because I am a firm believer that you get back what you put out into the world. Whether it's a positive or negative mindset, what you put out into the world is what you will receive back in return. I also value my sincerity because we all make decisions whether good or bad. But I want all of my decisions to be of sound judgement. Although very simple, these are very important characteristics missing in young men in the urban community. You are what you're taught . People will aspire to be what they emulate around them or their communities. The exploitation of youth and their lack of knowledge to know that they are in more control then they think of their current situation. The options to make it out are focused on the easy way as opposed to the road less traveled , the hard way of doing things. But in reality , nothing worth having ever comes easy!

Growing up in my household , often we watched the local news on channel 12. It kept us informed of what was going on in the tristate area (NJ,NY,CT). It would be on in the morning as I enjoyed my cereal an at night shortly before bedtime. My grandma was always informed on her current events. By seeing the news each day , I noticed at a young age. The terrible things occurring in not only my area but the surrounding inner city neighborhoods as well. If I thought things were bad, others clearly had it worse. I felt remorse for the families who lost loved ones. It also created fear of someday being a victim myself if I didn't move right.

I was born and raised in similar circumstances as some of the victims and suspects. I had to walk the same streets each day from school, play at the same parks, live in the same housing complex. I was aware that the streets weren't the place for me though. But how did I combat "The belly of the beast"? My solution was good character. By not only making one or two good decisions but by making a lifestyle out of being a good genuine individual with character. You only have one chance to make a first impression. I always made sure that first impression would be the best because I had control over that. Having good character has opened the door for great friendships. Business partnerships, healthy relationships. Could we agree that good character isn't being taught the way it was in the good old days.

Young me each day are learning when it's too late, making mistakes they wouldn't have made if they had better judgement. This book is titled Makings of a Man. Because becoming a man happens overtime, certain experiences mold you for better or worse. Just the same way certain ingredients add flavor to a dish when made properly , but over indulgence in anything unnecessary can ruin things. I want young men to know that they are a work in progress. Acquiring the right character traits along the journey will make you a complete man . By having confidence when life demands it of you . Self – awareness to know yourself , what good and bad for your well –being. Honesty and displaying humility when its required. If we are able to stand up each time life knocks you down . We are capable of reaching our very best potential. We are all capable of great things, but just like every high rise eve built . It all starts with a strong foundation. Character is that foundation

3 CONFIDENCE

-A feeling of self – assurance arising from one's appreciation of one's abilities or qualities.

When you look in the mirror. What do you see? Have you set goals and dreamt of accomplishing them…is the person that you see in the mirror on his way toward accomplishing these goals, or is he on the wrong path, totally off course?

Life is 10% what you experience & 90% how you respond to it.

Dorothy M. Neddermeyer

To be completely honest, for a while the reflection I did see actually was headed into the wrong direction. But it was the confidence in myself and my abilities that assured me, no matter how far I ventured off track . I could turn it all around once my focus was set on the right things.

To me , confidence isn't something you wake up with. It's something that is acquired over time through many trials and tribulations. My childhood is a testament to that and my adult life as well in so many ways. I always tell people "I wasn't the best at anything, but what I did know was, in due time with hard work I would be better. If I kept at it, I would do better, be better, understand better whatever it was that I was doing. They say "Knowledge is Power"! It truly is because whether in sports or the workforce. Whoever has the greater understanding of a given tasks, always completes the task better.

My journey to find my confidence began young . As a kid without any experience , I in some ways forged the opportunity to play Pop Warner football for the local youth team Elizabeth Giants. I say forged because at the age of 11 I did just that. My best friend Julio was very athletic and active. His mom Theresa and Julio were and still are the greatest most supportive parents I've known and someday hope to raise children with their love and care, but back to the subject. My best friend had begun playing football , so every time I would go over to see if he could come outside to play or have company. Mrs. Theresa would tell me that he had gone to practice.

One day I expressed interest to big Julio and he got me a Participation Slip and told me the cost would be $60.00 and I needed a physical from a doctor. Ok now I had a mission to complete. My mom was young and didn't understand a lot that was going on so I took it upon myself to just sign the slip and forge her signature in the best cursive I knew how to write. Second objective was to figure out how I was going to get $60.00 , that was the equivalent to 250.000 dollars today, Now that I sit and think about it. My uncle lived with us and had been a small time drug dealer. I knew where he kept a stash of money . So me and my brother set out to take a small portion of it and split it. My brother hid his portion and I hid mine. My uncle would later come home and whoop us. My brother would confess where he hid his portion, but I kept quiet. With paper signed and cash ready, I presented this to my friends dad, he knew of a clinic and I went by myself and before you knew it I was square away to play.
Quick Disclaimer – What I did to my uncle was totally wrong and I

wouldn't suggest anyone to do what I did ever. Just at the time it was the only way I knew how to get it as honest as possible.

Coming into my first few practices I didn't know how organized football was played but I had an eagerness to learn. All I knew was there were two sides – Offense & Defense. Gym class taught me that the offense attempted to score and were made up many positions. Wide Receiver , Running Back and most important position on offense was the Quarterback. Defense was pretty much straight forward. Anyone not on offense attempting to score, we're doing the opposite. Keeping the opposing team from scoring.

So from my lack of understanding the game in its entirety , playing a organized form of it was a completely different world for me. An I didn't have too much guidance to teach me the ropes. Everything was learned through trial and error and a valid effort to not makes the same mistakes twice.

My first time being hit really hard taught me to protect myself. My first few times missing a tackle taught me how to break down and tackle correctly .

In and throughout my childhood, I learned from my failures and those failures made me better. I once heard that new skills are acquired through repetitions. Once you've developed over time a high volume of repetitions , it becomes a Skill!

I was always honest with myself about my situation and my football abilities. I was well aware of what I was up against, which were the negative influences in the neighborhood, the gangs, the corners & especially the women that made that life seem appealing. So I rather be home than outside. Instead of making the same mistakes as everyone else. I often say to myself' What if I decided the negative route, I could've been a street legend." I was smart , I was calculated but it dawned on me, to live in the streets, seemed like a easy route. I wanted to travel the road less traveled and make something of myself. Too many examples of what not to be, becoming a positive role model became very appealing to me. If I continue to protect myself and work hard I could be just as good as anyone at my age in any sport in due time.

I was just as strong, just as fast . It was just my lack of knowledge of the game at that moment. So after my first few years of playing pop warner, being somewhat a bench warmer. I learned a lot, I saw the game from the outside looking in and learned a lot from what coaches call "Mental Reps". I saw the way things played out so many times on the field, that when my opportunity came , I felt like I had been there before, I was confident in getting the job done. So when Middle school came I was finally a Starter, playing both offense and defense (Linebacker & Fullback). Now that I was in a position to play more, I had to obtain the confidence to lead. I had to lead my fellow teammates to victory. Looking to my left and right with the confidence that my teammates will be their job done and I would too. The first few years were a great learning experience for me. In middle school I learned that I was an extremely hard hitter. I was capable of hitting the bigger and fastest guys on the field with a hit they would never forget. This confidence came from me believing and saying to myself. " If I would be willing to step to any individual big or small outside of this equipment. I had to keep that same energy with the equipment on. I wasn't intimidated and I believed everyone was a target.

During my freshman year of high school I started fullback and linebacker. I was confident and able to excel at the positions because of all the years I played football at the same position. I acquired knowledge and techniques that help me stand out. I knew what speed and strength the position demanded of me So preparation became key: lifting weights each day with my teammates, running track in the offseason to improve my speed. I began all of this preparation so that when the opportunity came , I possessed the confidence and skill to perform.

During my sophomore year of high school . The former coach Wiener retired after a few successful years. I was fighting for a spot on the varsity football team, of a high school that had about 5,000 students attending. The opportunity to make the team and play couldn't have been any slimmer. That year Elizabeth Board hired a new coach by the name of Chet .P. A great coach that had once been name by Joe.P as one of the greatest linebackers out of Penn State University. Penn State was one of the best line backing schools in the country. Coming into a urban city he knew we were hungry. He was confident as a coach he had the knowledge to get us there. With his coaching, our eagerness to learn and make something of ourselves, we formed one of the greatest championship teams Elizabeth has ever seen. Winning all but one game and winning the North 2 Group 4 Championship. That is one of the greatest accomplishments of my life. My senior year I took all that I learned while being a part of this championship team and applied it toward leading my team to a playoff berth. I was confident I possessed the skills to play at the next level. I went on to play football at American international college, I played the same positions throughout this experience. In grad school at AIC, I played rugby as well , with the knowledge I obtained with my years playing football , I applied it to certain aspects of my rugby career.

Do you notice the trend here?

Confidence is the result of experience, repetition and determination you can get something done. One's belief in themselves, that any goal can be accomplished because you've been there before in your own way and you've come out victorious no matter the situation whether it is in everyday life or sports , you just have to find that correlation.
Your confidence I would say is the voice of your heart speaking to you , telling you what you truly believe you can do.

4 SELF - AWARENESS

- Is the capacity for introspection and the ability to recognize oneself as an individual separate from the environment and other individuals.

When I discover who I am, I'll be free

Ralph Ellison

We all grow up with self-awareness issues. Have you ever been mad ,but haven't been able to pin point why you're mad or upset (Mood Swings) ? Have you ever overacted to a very small issue? That's because we all have issues that we haven't dealt with, or issues we really haven't recognized as issues because they seem manageable and we think were ok, or we don't know they exist yet.

When I was a teenager I myself realized living situation wasn't the best . I realized I wasn't the best in any sport or academics, But I was able to critique myself and figure out what it is or was that I like ,opposed to the other kids. Call me crazy but at times I looked in the mirror and talked to myself, I told myself what I did good and I told myself what I did bad or what I needed to improve upon. Because when you have a mom that doesn't understand everything you're going through, and a father that's absent . An that's the case in most urban families. The mirror became my best friend, & it should become yours too ,because in it was someone you couldn't lie to, myself!

The mirror knew my strengths and all my weaknesses. The mirror never told me what I wanted to hear, but it did show me who I was & that's all needed to know. I couldn't lie to it, because I am that person in it . So before we take this any further I want you to look in the mirror and remember the picture I told you to paint of yourself. Really ask the mirror, am I really working toward making this picture a reality. Am I happy where I am today? Does what I plan on doing tomorrow help me get closer to achieving my goals? Self-Awareness is accepting the fact that although you're in the same place as everyone else, you're still an individual with your own thoughts and ideas.

A follower lives life by what his surroundings says is cool and acceptable. He lets other dictate the actions of his life. A leader lives his life knowing, where he or she is today is only temporary. A leader has a plan because they know there is always work to be done and progress to be made. Take what it is that you're good at and become better in everything you lack, work to become good at. Never be content or comfortable because no matter what, life doesn't stop and there is still so much more to be accomplished. You're not in a competition with anyone else but yourself ,Life isn't a race but a Marathon ,and you're competing against yourself .. No one can hold you back, Only Yourself . An same person can only push you forward.

Good ..Better….BEST!

5 HUMILITY

-A modest or low view of one's own importance, humbleness.

On the highest throne in the world, we still only sit
on our bottoms

Michel De Montaigne

I was far from humble entering college, I had a chip on my shoulder from high school, because although I was on a championship team my junior year . I felt as though I didn't earn that ring. Even after a senior year campaign as a starter and captain. Making the playoffs in one of the most competitive conferences (Watchung Conference). I still felt as though I had skills and abilities that were not being acknowledged. I could never get over the hump and tap into my true potential. Always the thought that I was falling short of great but I was just good enough. My ego was sensitive in a sense, like I had the willing power and determination to win like Mayweather. But on the other end, what people thought and said about me actually bothered or hurt me. I cared too much about what others thought about me .

At the end of my senior season nothing had been going as planned. I was face to face with disappointment, no scholarship offers, I didn't know what was next for me. But with much help from my high school principal at the time Mr.Marque. He helped me sign up for my SAT's, he helped me put together a highlight film. An also helped me to package and distribute my highlight tape to any and every school I could think of. If your reading this Mr. Marque, I'm greatly appreciative of you and your efforts in my life. You def. set the bar in my life of what a man is. After all of our efforts. I eventually ended up at American International College. There I quickly excelled on the football field, I brought a level of intensity unmatched by my peers. My freshman year on the field I initially rotated with the starts on defense during Spring-ball. My sophomore year was my freshman year on the field and I had been transferred over to offense to play a Fullback position. I started fullback that year and was pretty confident that I had secured myself a scholarship after the season ended.

The fact that I had come from a low income home, made me eligible for grants and much help from the state funding which man school very affordable without any scholarships. So at the end of the season I thought I established myself enough , starting in front of a few of my schools scholarship investments at my same position. To be a freshman on the field and actively see the field on a team made up of a majority upper class-men. That was a big deal! I assumed my coaches saw in me, what I saw in myself , great potential moving forward!

On multiple occasions the head coach asked me to bring him my ledger (Tuition Bill) . I was sure financial assistance was soon to come. So I let things be and assumed my duties on the team. The next season I retired for camp and before your allowed to participate in camp. You had to make sure everything was squared away with the financial aid office. As I paced to

20

the office, I never felt more confident in my life that everything was going to be great. I was thought this was a quick visit but then it happened. "Jalil you have an remaining balance, how do you want to take care of this"?

"What?" I then asked if anything in my ledger was money from a football scholarship? "Maybe if didn't update or something." Nothing!" She replied with a look of disappointment for me. See I was very close with the ladies in the finance department because they knew I took care of everything by myself. My mom and no-one in my immediate family understood college or due processes involved. So in my family, I was the pioneer to the college world. I was devastated and hurt but I loved football. So I proceeded to camp and once again established myself as a valuable part of the team. But when things financially didn't go right. I quit the team. The following year, I came out , It's my junior year , and once again I'm a starter without any financial aid. So I quit again, My senior year, I was prepared to put my pride to the side and just not only become a starter, but actually finish the season out. I was determined but here was a game I loved, a game that has contributed so much to my growth and maturity. It was almost like loving someone, that didn't love you back at this point. I

I without a doubt had the respect of my peers, my teammates but I couldn't understand what was going on in the coaches office. Before the season started we had a team scrimmage and I still received the short end of the stock. I then let my emotions get the best of me, an while enraged I approached my coach to have a conversation to try and understand my situation. But my emotions got the best of me and I went on to quit.

When I look back at this experience I regret it because I wish I finished. In all of the things I've ever done in my life, this was on things I loved and let go. I remember a conversation with my good friend Dan .P , he was the second string quarterback and our current starter was a stud.
Anyone who knows football knows how hard it is to be a backup quarterback when the starter is in your same class. You almost never see the field and you play the role of supporting cast majority of the games. But throughout his situation. He remained humble and did everything that he could to contribute to the team . I recall ranting to him and stating how much I'm better than other guys on the team etc. he went on to reply with one word "Humility".

My mind went racing "What was Humility?" I knew humble to an extent and I knew what humiliate meant but these words together. What was this? He went on to say it again. "Jalil you need to learn Humility, What was that? I was so confused so I googled the word. Humility is the act of thinking less of yourself and just being humble. Knowing what your capable of and just letting the work speak for itself and making the most of every given opportunity shouldn't been my mindset.

If I simple stuck it out in these situations. Things would've swing in my favor eventually. There were moment I just wasn't ready for. I once read that good things don't occur when you want them to happen. They actually occur when you're ready for them. When the timing is right! That conversation made me look back to a time of my life when I witnessed my grandma lose her jobs a teacher's aide. A test came out that she just couldn't pass because she was so far removed from school. All she knew was how to do her job, and she was really good at it, taking care of special ed kids in kindergarten. She loved her job but she loved those kids even more. After numerous tries at the test she was reduced from a teacher's aide to a lunch lady. Going from a classroom to serving food in a kitchen.

That transition was embarrassing for her , but I remember her being in her room and studying each night. Attempting to take and pass that test every chance she got. Although she never passed that test she never quit her job. Maybe that was a sign for me while in high school of things to come. She never quit so I should never quit regardless of my situation. Me quitting that many times not only hurt myself but my teammates and possible relationships.

I brought something to the team in my other abilities, not starting offense or defense but my special teams presence. Quitting will be something I 'll always regret because it lingered with me for a while and once you've quit one thing you think its ok to do it with other things when you should have been resilient . I had good jobs and instead of sticking it out I quit. I didn't feel like Jalil again until I finished College. It was only then that I felt back on track. I went through something, I finished and remained humble along the way.

You will face hardships and you will see glory. Being humble and hardworking in both stages is the key to life.

6 WOMEN

-An adult human , a wife, girlfriend, lover , a grandmother, mother , aunt, niece , sister , cousin.

Every Woman is a Queen

...

So many titles in your family that you can think of to name this beautiful being that god has created to be a companion to man. When I was young I vividly remember a conversation with my uncle in which he stated, "This is a woman's world, we just live in it." I didn't gasp the concept of what he was saying but throughout my life I was always reminded of the importance of women to our society. Whether it is a Tupac poem/song. Beyoncé's "Who runs the world campaign or Formation.

To even the Kardashian Family. I've always been reminded how powerful women are and respected them. But little did I know the power that a woman can have over a man. My success in life is credited a lot to my own ambitions and myself. But at the end of the day, to be honest what drove me to becoming more than I was in the past was Heartache. Yes, I said it, having that heartbroken a couple of times or even once will either make or break a man. It makes you look at yourself and ask what's wrong with me? Am I not good enough, a thousand and one things can go through your mind. Were taught so much in this lifetime but not how to love and control those powerful emotions.

Feelings are the hardest thing to deal with if you aren't experienced in dealing with them. One lesson I've learned. Just because it doesn't work out, it doesn't mean that it's the end of the world. It's just the end of a chapter in your life. But a lot of men don't realize this because it's a lesson not taught often but rather experienced. A powerful experience even compared to that of a traumatic experience I'd say. Women are raising men in today's society more often than usual alone. For a while in my life I blamed men for not being there for their children, then it dawned on me, for these women to have these children by these men, they had to choose them. Now these are things that you don't realize until you're an adult and unhappy I realized this as a young guy.

Those good guys really do finish last, but the difference between a bad man and a good man is. A good man always finishes! Let that sink in. There are different types of men; a woman has a huge responsibility in choosing the right one. Mr. Right isn't always Mr. Right, he can be Mr. wrong in disguise or etc. a good man may come in the form of a bad guy. A woman will never know but at the end of the day. A woman makes the decision. Woman still don't realize the power over man that they have. But you young man can realize today how powerful they are and respect it and be aware. Don't love a woman until your truly ready. Don let your friends alter how you feel about women.

An most importantly treat women how you would want a man treating the women in your family. I noticed the absence of men in my family. So growing up I wanted to be everything they weren't. A Man! A respected man not just by other men but women as well. A man known to pursue all of his goals and if I ever indulged in getting a woman pregnant. Having the courage to step to the plate, be a provider and start a family. Find Mrs. Right and keep her, love her and cherish her. Treat women like the queens they are and the women that chose to be otherwise, let them be that. It isn't your job or duty in any form to judge someone else. Just be aware. Just make sure to make yourself happy and love yourself before you go out loving everyone else. I comes before them because if you don't have things in order. Nobody is going to do it for you,

7 FAMILY

— *All descendants of a common ancestor*

The most important thing in the world is Family & Love

John Wooden

Being African American or whatever decent you are the ancestors the greats and the grand's have gone through so much for you to exist. Whether it is during the early times enduring and surviving slavery or modern times. Establishing themselves the best way they knew how during segregation. To today's world sacrificing their childhoods as young parents to raise a family. Family is so important that you owe it to all of those before you to be great. Family is all that exist when all is gone. They are the people that will love you unconditionally and you will love them the same. The only people in this world that are supposed to care. Your last name means a lot,

Represent it well. I can recall so many times where Family played a huge impact in my life. Growing up my mom was an alcoholic, I was young and needed guidance but there was only so much my Grandma and Aunt could do. I recall a period where protective child services came and split our family up for a short period of time. My grandma was living with her sister Aunt Nadine on Anna Street and on top of her apartment my grandmas other sister Aunt Peggy lived on top of her. Aunt Nadine lived alone and Aunt Peggy lived with her Husband Uncle OC and my cousin Shavell. Shavell was my age well around the same age about 2 years older. Moving in, I didn't have much, but my cousin had everything, all the coolest sneakers and she was a girl but she bought all of her stuff in boy sizes. An the boy sizes she happen to get was my size.

It's so crazy because the timing was perfect. I was in middle school, a time in life where social status mattered to a young kid, she would look at my outfit every morning before school and if she didn't like the sneakers I had on. She would give me a pair of her latest Jordon's or Nikes or Converse to wear. At that age I learned the importance of family and selflessness. She cared too much for me to go out looking any kind of way.

Because when I stepped outside, I not only represented myself but I represented her as well. I was Shavell's little cousin. I was Gail's grandson, and Aunt Nadine's and Aunt Peggy's Nephew. It made me look at the world different. I began to live like when I walked outside the door, I represented my family, so every time I'm outside, I need to represent in the best way possible and do nothing to disrespect myself or my last name. With that attitude I avoided so many potholes and obstacles of the everyday urban community. I never joined a gang, didn't steal ever. I was on a mission in life to enjoy life and go out and accomplish things no one in my family has done yet because my accomplishments weren't just mine, they were my families as well. Toward my senior year of high school I didn't have the money to pay to take my SATS over and over.

It was about $60 bucks to take an exam and it was a test I needed to take over because I needed a certain score. I wasn't working at the time; I was just focused on sports and getting better. I was big on sacrifice and I figured if I scarified what everyone else wanted "Today" it would set me up for a brighter future and a better tomorrow. I remember telling my cousin Amirah my situation.

The next day my Aunt Peggy her grandmother told me Amirah had giving her money so that I could take my SAT again. That's what family is for, she saw my potential and knew I needed the help, she was my age in the same grade, but in that moment she became my little big cousin. I was inspired to never let her down. An I didn't, when I took the exam for the last time, I got the score I needed and moved on to college.

My cousin Amirah today has obtain her doctorate degree, I have my MBA, and Family made this happen. In Sports before my football games I would get my wrist taped up and on them In magic marker I would write the initials of all the people in my immediate family. To someone randomly looking at my wrist, it would look like a bunch of gibberish but to me it meant everything. It's what did and always will get me through the fourth quarter. In college, in life family becomes your biggest support system. I recall numerous nights where my younger cousins or sister would order me food because I was hungry and chasing a dream. I would call Aunt Keisha and Aunt Keisha would always say, "call Kabriya, Aliyah, Janae. Her daughter and my cousins. We were all brought up as Sisters and brothers cause our mothers were siblings.

I thought I had the roughest life at one point but now that I look at it. I didn't, I was rich in Family. Not monetary things, Family! I had a whole network of cousins, aunts etc. that I could depend on and most importantly my mother. Although she had her own vices. I don't think no other woman could have raised me the way she did. What I experienced living in my household made me such a strong man. I don't regret anything; yes I wished things were different. But we took the cards we were dealt and played them well.

I had nothing but my family and wanting better for them, motivated me to go out and get everything! I was a positive guy and focused on accomplishing so much. But I knew someday my faith would be tested. I was a few weeks away from completing my undergrad experience when I came home to go out with friends for a night of partying and drinking etc. I never made it to the bar and that night ended up in jail with a 1,000,000 bond. Because of family, that bail was reduced and because of my cousins research I happened to find the best lawyer to represent me.

My cousin Antoinette stepped to the plate when I hadn't seen her in years. She was the daughter of my Aunt Joyce, my grandmas other sister. Yes my grandma has a lot of sisters and brothers loll. But my cousin Antoinette when she was younger worked as a paralegal and she had knowledge well more than everyone else in the family of the current situation and the severity as well. She started a GoFundMe page to help in efforts to raise bail money for me. She also communicated with my school to let them know the situation and got documents prepared as needed for my lawyer. It was a blessing to have my cousin step into my life and take over the time that she did and I'll always be grateful for that. I not only got out of jail but completed my coursework when the semester was over. And went on to complete grad school as well and get my master's degree. Family got me here. Family will be there when it matters most and hold your hand through the darkest times in life and be there to celebrate by your side when the light shines. I share this to say this, your family deserves for you to go out and represent each other in the best way possible. I understand were all freethinkers and really should go out and live life to the fullest but also think. IF you do negative things in the world, your family made inherit consequences that weren't meant for them. Family is everything.

8 PERSISTENCE

-Continuing firmly or obstinately in a course of action in spite of difficulty or opposition.

-Continuing to exist or endure over a prolong period.

Ambition is a path to success. Persistence is the vehicle you arrive in .

Bill Bradley

Another essential characteristic in the structure of manhood is Persistence, having the confidence to believe in yourself is the first steps in achieving your goals, but how many times are you willing to fall and get back up, fail and try again. Keep pushing even though things aren't going your way. Simply being born with a gift doesn't mean that it will manifest and be perfected just because of your natural abilities.

Gifts need to be nurtured, work needs to be done; effort needs to be initiated to meet potential. Life is one huge journey, we all have capabilities for a reason, and you never know what skill you naturally have that will make you into the man you were meant to be. You want to know who's persistence, Sean Puffy Combs, in my eyes this man has weathered so many storms but somehow someway he prevails every time. The East/West beef. The JLo/Shyne club situation.

Throughout all the hardships. This man continues to remain relevant in the game. I use him as an example because sometimes you just have to push through hard times. I look at any hardship or goal like it's a tunnel and every tunnel has its dark moments. But you can rest assure that at the end of that tunnel is an exit and a sun that's patiently waiting to shine so bright upon you. I learned in life that things don't happen overnight, or in a day or two. To make real changes in your life, you have to commit to them, this decision must become a lifestyle, a new way of living. For example someone looking to become physically fit. They can't go to the gym one day out of the week and expect to be fit. They must go 3,4,5 days of the week. They must fall in love with the feeling of ripping and expanding their muscles. They must embrace the feeling of pain after a long day of work. To be great at anything in life it takes persistence. Life is filled with so many obstacles, so many things that although seem very harmless can steer anyone of us off of our path to greatness. Dig deep and figure out what you want out of life, remember the picture you painted. Now let's continue to take steps toward achieving it each and every day.

What have you done so far to get closer to making your dreams a reality? List key accomplishments (Degrees, Certifications, Etc.)

List what you need to accomplish

Remembering all the while, the plan you chose to put in action, you must push forward and remain consistent & persistent throughout. Every day is a day you can use to get better and closer to achieving your goals.

So tell me what is your game plan?

Where are you in life and where do you want to take things in the next 5 years. (This is your chapter)

Say it right now, say it in this book!

Jalil Q. Oates

9 DISAPPOINTMENT

-The feeling of sadness or displeasure caused by the nonfulfillment of one's hopes or expectations.

We must accept finite disappointment, but never lose infinite hope

Martin Luther King Jr.

That hope that things would go your way but when all the smoke clears. The result you expected doesn't occur. We've all been there and I'm here to tell you that disappointment is a part of success. It goes hand and hand like the good and the bad. But what you do when disappointed will play a huge impact on how much you succeed. Disappoint to me is like the fuel to the fire, the logs that were meant to burn.

Growing up I've had my fair share of disappointment but now that I look back, they all made me a better man. I vividly remember my mom bringing me to see my Dad face to face. He gave me a number, which now I realize was a beeper number. Wow if I meant that much to him he would've gave me a direct line or something. But I beeped him the following day and after a few times, he gave me a call back. He told me that he'd pick me up later. To have some man time, you know him, and me a day out the house in my eyes. Similar to what my brother was getting with his dads family. He told me around 5:5:30 he'd be outside and for me to be ready. So when 5 came around,
I was packed and ready. 5:15, still no sign of him but he told me 5-530.

After hours of waiting outside my mother finally came downstairs to get me. The whole while she had been watching me from upstairs as I sat on the steps telling all my friends from the building I'm waiting for my daddy. Something tells me that my mom knew he wasn't coming but it was just something I had to see for myself. And that day I did, I cried my eyes out but on that day something happened to me. I vowed never to be the same man he was, people told me stories about how he was this and that, which made me want to be the total opposite. A most importantly if I ever was a father, I would be the best dad in the world and give my children all of my time and everything it is that I have to offer. Being disappointed made me better. I think of all of the different speeches and motivational talks where they point out that before Michael Jordan made all of those clutch great shots. He missed a good number of them first. Very few are born into glory but for the most part. We all know what the bottom, taste, smells, feels like.
The energy of disappointment is very negative, but we have an option as to what we want to do with that energy. We can apply it toward something negative in life and unbeneficial, living a life of using disappointment and traumatic experiences as an excuse. Or we can rise above it and say to ourselves. This is the result today but it won't is that next time. In sports I've always been on the side of the team winning by huge margins or a lot of points. Until one day I was on the opposite side, my team getting our ass whooped and losing by 45 points. There's nothing you can do but endure it. But something happened during that lost. Although we were losing really

badly, I wanted to finish; I wanted to see things through to the end. That my friends is where heart set in and was on display. In life things aren't supposed to go our way, but it's how we react, my mother passed away the day before Mother's day and that was the hardest thing I ever had to deal with. I had so many hopes and dreams of what I wanted to do for her. Looked forward to her being a grandparent to my beautiful kids. Award ceremonies etc.

Then when she passed away, all of those special moments faded away as well. I'll live a lifetime of heartache, but instead of being down and staying down. I knew she wanted more for me. At a young age she sacrificed so much to give me a chance at life, I owed her to show her that those sacrifices were worth it. I took all the heartache and pain and applied that energy towards something positive; the thought of disappointing her propelled me to new heights in life. I finished Grad School when I didn't think I had it in me. I survived the dark days but when I think about it all. The dark days contributed just as much to the success as the good days.

The hard times taught me so much because I allowed them to be my teacher. Rather than rebelling against them. Tough times do not last at all, like they say, pain is temporary. When I finished grad school I was under the impression that I would be getting brand new car for all of the things I've accomplished . My godmother was like my second mom and whatever my mom couldn't do . She was right there and always took care of things. My god mom Shaun was a detective in Elizabeth .

So you know she was a very firm woman and used every chance she could to teach me a lesson in all my mistakes. If they ever say women can't raise men I'll call "Bull crap" because she was the most independent woman I've ever met.

Just before grad school ended my Aunt Keisha told me my god mom may be buying me a car. I was so excited and told all my friends . I never had a car and looked so forward to it . Visualizing myself stunting and blasting music along the main streets of my city . Pulling up to the clubs etc. Then the day came when I was at her house and she told me that I'd be taking the car parked in the driveway. It was a beat down civic that had been sitting there the last two years.

I was so hurt and disappointed. I viewed the car as a slap in the face , to me it was the equivalent of me doing one year of college and dropping out and saying "Hey I tried". Me and her had a falling out over this and my attitude toward the situation . But I didn't realize what she was really preparing me for . The real world! Not having an insurance payment , not having a car note. But having a car that I owned and could drive to and from work each day until I saved enough to afford a nicer car.

I wish every day that I took that car.

10 FRIENDSHIP

- Look around yourself; are the people you hang with on the daily basis helping you in any way to make your dreams a reality? Do they play a major part in your life? Do they make you truly happy? At a young age, we all have such a hard time defining what true friends and friendship is… We naturally want to be surrounded by the coolest friends, the prettiest girls. But will they really be the coolest people to be around. Someone once said in a movie to "Monetize your friendships."

My best friend is the one that brings out
the best in me

Henry Ford

If there not propelling you forward and you doing the same for them. You have no use for one another in the long run. But when your young that means nothing, we all have childhood friends, but this is the best timing to begin making good friends.

Don't be the coolest kid in the class, or the bully. Be the good kid that laughed and respected everyone. You never know who could be the best friend for you, you never know who your best suited to be friends with. The weird kid everyone says jokes about may like all the games and shows you like. What you lack are his strengths and what he lacks you can help him out.

That's what true friendship is, being there for one another and making each other better people. Women can also be really good friends because they know and see things from a totally different perspective then men. So don't go out trying to have sex with every girl that thinks your cool. The friend zone can actually benefit you. Surround yourself with people that won't lead you down the wrong path toward negativity, surround yourself with people that want what you want in life and are doing what you're doing. Always be honest with your friends and loyal. Lying to people and betraying them makes you an untrustworthy individual and no one wants to be around disloyal people except other disloyal individuals. Always be sincere, don't do things to people just to get ahead.

Things may be bad today but they won't last forever. But back to the young kid living in the projects. Where everyone is either selling drugs or gang banging. How does he become self-aware and separate himself from the norms of the environment. At first I didn't know, but then I noticed from watching the news, it's all a cycle, be out there die, or go to jail then the next kids turn and the next kids turn. I first learned to break that cycle by separating myself, why subject yourself to something that you're scared of. I was scared of the streets, the violence, and the death that came along with it. So I surrounded myself with others that felt the same way. We all were willing to protect ourselves. But that was trouble we didn't look for. We didn't want what we saw each and every day on the streets or the news.

We wanted to go to school and make it home, play at the park and make it home. I never wanted to hang on the block etc. I knew my place and that wasn't it. But I still didn't know myself until I was exposed to other things. At a young age I was introduced to Pop Warner football my first sport and still I wasn't good. Got my 10 plays a game and out my first year.

I came home one night and the guys on the block recognized my helmet. It was a Dookie, which is a football helmet with the bar in the middle. The guys outside looked at my helmet and laughed at it. So it made me aware that I wasn't the best on the field, I was a lineman, wasn't one of the special players. So right then I knew I was at the bottom and there was work to be done. But I also knew it was my first year playing a sport and each year would be a learning experience. I wasn't scared of the journey, I didn't have born skills and I think that's the best thing that ever happened to me. I had to work for everything nothing was given. But often in the neighborhood there are young men born with natural born talent and it all just goes to waste. That's due to lack of guidance, When father figures are missing, It leaves women to raise boys to men the best way they know how. A some women do a great job but some women just aren't fit to raise boys into men.

A son being able to provide for the family with drug money, not all mothers are stopping there kids because majority of women enjoy being spoiled by a man with fast money. In most urban communities, this kids father was a drug dealer, his uncles do the same. Even the mother's father was probably a drug dealer too. It's a cycle that I noticed and wanted to break. Me and my older brother both had dads that were incarcerated for similar crimes, drugs, etc. My brother wanted to be just like his father. I wanted to be a Man! I realized my dad was absent and his actions taking the negative route were the reason why he wasn't able to be a part of my life, or absent for so long. His mistakes made me want to become everything that he wasn't for me. But if I'm ever to be a good father, and a husband someday how do I make it out? Young men were dying every week; outside on the streets I had to walk to and from school each day.

Then in middle school I met my best friend and his family. They lived in a house with a backyard with a pool and basketball court. It was right around the corner from my building I loved it. His dad and mom were married, they had their own car to get back and forth to work and drop the kids off to school. In my mind this was what being rich was, they had things I've never seen. Every gaming system that came out, every Christmas the tree loaded with gifts, dinner was always amazing, Being exposed to this family made me want my own family someday and even make my family better. But I realized although we were only blocks apart we lived in two separate worlds. My best friends Dad were a Man, he worked hard, long hours at his job and he was able to provide for his family. No man told me this growing up, I was only 10 and I already had friends who had running's with the law etc. But Julio was different; he was focused on sports because his family kept him away from all the negative things going on. No one kept me away from none of the negativity, I was experiencing it front row. So I knew now I had to move different. Although I lived in that world, I had to separate myself from it as much as possible.

My outlet was going to my best friend's house and doing the things a kid my age should be doing. I realized a man works hard and provides for his family and sets goals and achieves them. The drug dealers outside sold all day and lived in apartments, my friend's dad worked all day and lived in a beautiful house. I learned a woman as well works hard and provides for her family the best way she can, making sure the kids get to school and back, making dinner each night, being loving and caring. Being exposed to this family made me want so much more for my family and myself. The things my family lacked or the guidance I lacked I gained in that household. An that's the beginning of the journey toward making it out. Separating yourself and being around like-minded individuals. Don't surround yourself with the coolest kids from the neighborhood; surround yourself with the kids that enjoy doing the simple things that you do. Because Friendship plays a key role in you becoming successful someday.

So know what is that you actually want for yourself because there is so much you can accomplish. I knew if I wanted a good job someday I needed to make it out of elementary school, middle school, high school. If I wanted a good paying job I had to take that extra mile and make it to college and finish and for a even better paying job grad school. When you come from nothing you should want everything, when you have it all you should want to work hard to maintain it. It was a rough journey but that picture in my head was painted and along the journey the mirror image I saw I was proud of. Choosing the right friends can open the door to so much more.

Some of the young gentleman and women reading this book have made decisions in their life that they feel like 'Hey, I've already made decisions in my life, things aren't going to change. Me for one, I've never been a dad, I've never been arrested and convicted and turned things around. I haven't been a successful business owner yet or made a million dollars. So I won't sit and elaborate on things I haven't experienced, but I've been blessed to meet people who have gone through different obstacles in life and have prevailed. I am one thing A Man, my life is a constant journey and today I am happy where I am still writing my story of life. But the next few chapters, I will invite a few of my good friends to elaborate and share their own personal experiences that helped them to become the great men they are today after the adversity they've faced. Life is all about energy and the positive energy we gain from one another. At some point in my life, I've gotten great energy from these individuals. That now I want to share with you and hopefully our story and the character traits that we have learned to respect and honor, have a great effect on your life.

11 Belief:

Trust, Faith , or confidence in someone or something.

Believe that life is worth living & your belief becomes the fact

William James

Jalil Q. Oates

Who can you trust to guide you in the right direction? Who loves you more than anyone and everyone else? Who knows your purpose on this earth, An everything about your endless untapped potential? Yes, it is God!

An I believe that Belief in a higher being is essential in keeping you in line with your goals of living a full healthy life in the realms of Mental ,Emotion, and Spiritually , I've had my own battles with Belief throughout my life but I've noticed the trend in my life as well.

I made my most mistakes when I didn't believe and I ventured off course doing and living my life by my own terms. See although somethings may satisfy your happiness or relieve pain temporary. Those things or actions always aren't the best choices of course.

Each day where faced with things that may occur throughout our day. These situations continuously put us in position to either make a right or wrong decision to the matter at hand. I like to think of it like this, from sunrise to sundown, the devil and god battle for my soul. In every situation I face throughout my day, to every reaction I chose to give someone. It's a constant fight between what's best for me and temporary solutions to long term issues.

I know Marijuana is bad for me, it does nothing for me, as it makes me completely unproductive, sleepy, tired. I've smoked and I'm totally unproductive for the rest of the high. I go out and party and although it's fun in the moment. Liquor and bottles of it in a club atmosphere are very expensive. So in order for me to indulge into it, I must spend money at times I don't have to spend at that rate. For instance, a bottle of Henny cost $30 in stores. In the club that same $30 bottle can cost you up to $200, $250.

Do you catch the trend here? Indulging in these things are negative, selfish decisions. Both actions whether I had been smoking or drinking, took something away from me. Whether it be my productivity for the day, or my pockets at night. Because believe me when I say, You don't need Marijuana to relax, and release tension or blow off some steam. What are healthy ways to do these things?

This is where belief comes into play. I'm the type of guy that takes any and everything personal whether it's a joke someone said to a comment someone would make about me. I know I'm not the best person in the world . Not the most consistent, persistent person. But I do believe life does happen to people. We do sometimes make bad decisions throughout our life and indulge in things that for a time do cloud our judgement. To be overwhelmed with tension or anxiety and feel that a drug alleviates that current mood. These thoughts come from lack of belief, not having the purist heart to not let negative thoughts or emotions to cloud our judgement.

Negativity and Bad thoughts weigh you down more than you think, they take away from your ultimate ingredient to living a full life. Which is your Happiness, you can't feel complete if you aren't happy. An you find this Happiness in everything when you chose to live without judgement and search for the best in people.

When things in life bring you down, Belief is that hope and faith that whatever is happening is to only make you stronger. Your god felt as though you were a little weak, what happening currently is only to make you strong. Because life is a journey, and it has more battles along the way that through this pain and healing today. You will be more prepared for mentally, physically and emotionally. Belief helped me to succeed in life. An push through when I saw no other way. In church my Uncle pastor OC Anderson once said" God gives his toughest battles to his toughest soldiers". I've always felt in and throughout my life, I've been one of his toughest soldiers, You should too..

During my Senior year of undergraduate school, I came home to party with my friends so I caught a train from school to his house to get ready. I was in the house for only fifteen minutes before a group of people came and robbed the house. Shortly after the robbery of the home, Police came and eventually locked up everyone in the house. I was innocent and although it was my first time ever being arrested. The police gave me and my friends all one million dollar bails. I was petrified but I knew I was innocent, I believed that this whole situation would work itself out.

Being brought up in the urban environment you naturally learn the codes of the streets and I was well aware of these rules while experiencing what I was going through. An my friends that I got mixed up with I had faith in them to stand up when the time was right and that's what they did. After going to court for a year, the first of each month being offered outrageous plea deals, First deal being to serve a 8 year jail term. It made me realize how many uneducated men, Who can't afford lawyers, get court appointed people to defend them who don't have their best interest at mind. This experience brought my family together at a time when I could never feel so distant from them. Just before this tragedy happened to me, My cousin Antoinette wasn't doing too well. She struggled with alcoholism, and depression for a while. But this situation brought her back out of the darkness. Because she knew she served a higher purpose. From raising money online for my bail after the bail reductions. To raising money for my lawyer and picking the best lawyer to defend me. You see god working here? See in my cousins younger years she was a paralegal and understood everything about the situation I was currently in. Her knowledge came at a crucial point in my life and I'm beyond thankful for her saving my life in so many ways.

In my most trying time don't regret anything about the situation no matter how unfair and unjust it may sound. I saw the positive things that were happening in and throughout the experience. At a time when I didn't see and feel the love from my family. My god put me in a position to be showered with it. I told him It wasn't there, and he showed me that it was and stronger than I ever could imagine.

Being incarcerated also helped me to appreciate the small things in life. Being locked up in room not knowing the time. Only what part of the day it is by the meal you were being served. Having your freedom restricted in a room the size of an average bathroom. In this position is where my faith in god was the strongest. I had to believe all of this was happening to me for an ultimate reason. To be here in a cell with a million dollar bail and be innocent and no one know. I prayed each morning and each night to pass times. An one day while on the phone with my uncle pastor OC. He told me that this is just a speed bump in the road.

See we made be living life too fast, beyond our means at times and things need to happen in our lives to pump our breaks in ways. I saw the message in this experience. I was living too fast, going clubbing, spending money I didn't have. It was god telling me to wake up and smell the coffee. Appreciate the small things because at the end of the day. Simply having your freedom is the ultimate treasure.

Don't wait till it's too late to learn the lesson. Smell the roses and tend the plant as well. Continue to water the plant and watch it prosper. Don't just watch its beauty for a day and pass it by. Each day our body, mind is spirit need to be cleansed, watered and refreshed. Our belief in our god is that tool for us. An without it we just continue to hold on to bad experiences. Bad thoughts, our hearts will be hardened and our souls uncleansed. Belief is at the core of everything, or happiness our confidence, our courage and most importantly our Character.

12 Redemption

- *The action of saving or being saved from sin, error, or evil.*

I don't believe the world is a particularly beautiful place, but I do believe redemption is possible

Colum McCann

In whatever you're going through, Can you see the light at the end of the tunnel? I will tell you from actual first-hand experience that there come times in life where you don't actually see the light at the end of the tunnel. An although your surrounded by complete darkness. You must believe that there is a light at the end of the tunnel. An at that moment, when you reach the light again. You've redeemed yourself.

Do you believe me when I say that you can actually lose yourself and find yourself, An actually find yourself to be smarter, wiser, bigger and stronger than you ever were before? But in order t redeem yourself you must have certain Characteristics in order already, those character traits are Disappointment, Confidence, Perseverance & Belief.

Disappointment simply because you just have to have the strength to face the truth, Say a expected result didn't occur, you have to be able to deal with the results. Facing disappointment is the perfect motivator for success. And a key ingredient so many others success stories. Just the simple thought of being disappointment or feeling disappointment fuels and a rage and mind state to work hard so you don't have to feel those feelings.

Confidence comes into play after disappointment because after accessing the disappointment at hand , You should have the confidence to look yourself in the mirror and say no matter how bad it is. "We've come from worse circumstances and made something of ourselves" this is just another journey, a path I must walk to live and learn and ultimately get where I'm going.

Then there's Perseverance which becomes useful because in any work you must possess the strength to endure. Think of some situations like a fight in the movie Rocky. Although Rocky trained hard, he endured some brutal beatings from great opponents . but at the end of those fights he ended up the winner. Sometimes win are beautiful experience and on the other hand some other battles are ugly and coming out simply with the win is all that matters. To bring back the Tunnel analogy. Sometimes all you see is darkness and continuing to work in it because you know if you continue to push forward. Light will eventually show its face. An last but not least , and most important is your Belief. You have to know the lesson being taught in the experience. You have to find the positivity in and throughout the negativity.

I believed at one point my life was like the Biblical Book of Job: To give you a quicks summary of this book of Job. It was a man that believed in god and to prove to the devil that this man was a true believer in Christ. God let the devil touch his life to see if he would turn again god and his faith. Job lost all of his crops, children and health . In and throughout all of this pain he endured that he didn't deserves. He continued to pray to god and never turned against him. An as a result God was proven right and granted Job everything he had lost, doubled! For everything he lost he received twice in return, From Land, to children to wealth to health. His children and children's children all lived to live long lives. I believed I was the current version of this story.

After my mom had passed away, I dealt with it by honoring her and pushing forward each day to complete my degree. A few months before her passing I had lost my Uncle OC , who was like a father and mentor to me throughout my life. My mother was my biggest fan and believed in me more than I believed in myself at times. Now that I look at it , I clearly know that it was her job to shower me with endless love. When I graduated College, I made the crazy decision to shut my brain completely off and party my savings away. I obtained a job straight out of college working at a youth program with kids that suffered with anger management from trauma in and throughout their childhoods. I obtained the job through previous experience working with juveniles while in college in Massachusetts.

I noticed in so many instances that I was a very emotional individual and these emotions would surface whenever id drink or smoke. I knew were my vices were and what was hurting me and instead of avoiding them. I over indulged in them for temporary fixes to long term problems. The same relief I felt from smoking and drinking I also got from attending the gym consistency but going to the gym required work and I wanted to be lazy. Because my entire life I had lifted , played sports, attended meetings, workout. My life had been in a constant rotation of in season offseason, in season , off season. I was tired of it and began to live my life recklessly. During this time working back home I was able to save up money to quickly finance my first car. A infiniti G37 , I loved this car and it contributed to more of the partying, Driving all over to drink and party in my new car. I eventually smartened up and traded it in for something more affordable. Which was a 2015 Nissan Altima. Still it was a good car and life was going good, Until I began to lose sight of my responsibilities.

At this time I had a car, an apartment, a good job and I was actually doing good with women. Had a beautiful , loving , caring, girlfriend. I thought I had it made and I was on cruise control. But this life I was living eventually caught up to me. It started with my car being repossessed the me losing my job then losing my apartment an in due time losing my girlfriend as well. This book was actually finished and I didn't have the means to pay and push this project forward. My life was at a standstill and after having my own place I found myself sleeping on a couch in my grandma's house.

So many morning it hurt to be in the position I was in, still hanging out each day and smoking and drinking, feeling bad for myself and then doing it all over again. Then I realized , I can't continue down this path. It took for me to realize how far I've actually come. I didn't just fall and lose everything I've worked for my entire life. My life was just on pause and only me , myself and I had the power to pick up the pieces. I decided to start from square one.

I believed in order to have a healthy mind, body and spirit. I had to start with myself. My grandmother only tolerated me being in her space for a few days before she unleashed on me. Each morning complaining about me being there and sleeping too late. It enraged me and before you knew it I was attending the gym each morning. I went every morning to avoid getting yelled out and I quit smoking and drinking for a while. I went to the gym each day morning. An once I built myself up mentally, I began going to the library after lifting and reading and applying to jobs.

One day while on social media I noticed a friend of mine suggested a book for other young men to ready. It was titled " Wild At Heart" an how we can find ourselves and true strengths in the midst of so much tragedy and confusion because men are more connected to the wild and free atmosphere of the forest than we think. I noticed the trend of the strength that can be acquired throughout adversity. I read the book while retreated for a weekend trip in NC at my friends Macky house.

While in NC, I witness the life my friend had been living. Sacrificing the fun and wild life I had been living to establish a successful business. This business being Brooklyn Brothers Pizza, In Asheville. It I've never ate a chicken parm till this day that compares to theirs. When I returned home I had a totally new attitude towards a lot of people and things. I eventually acquired a job at a temp agency. I would pay uber to get to and from work. An in most cases I spent money just to make money. Spending $30 to work and $30 from work. Just to build my confidence for finding a job. Putting myself back in that atmosphere, After a few really good assignments. I knew I was ready to work again. I applied to Enterprise rental and after a few really lengthy interviews, I was able to obtain a job as a Management trainee.

And after spending a month or two living with my grandma. I had found an apartment. So at this time I had a better job than the one I had lost making more money. An my new apartment was actually bigger than my last one. After a few months, I had saved up enough to purchase a black on black challenger. A car that months prior I made my screen saver on my phone. I had lost everything then gained it back better.

I was the book of Job in my own way. I felt the pain of disappointment, Disappointment in myself but I had confidence that although I lost it all I could get it back. I persevered through living with my grandma, taking ubers every day to work to make practically no money. But gain the necessary experience to push forward. I believed in myself and my god. That all of this was happening to humble me and see life and its worldly things for what they were just things. Appreciate the simple things in life and love those that deserved my love. I'm not perfect and you aren't either but whatever you're going through , you can get through. Things are going to knock you down, but you must have the inner strength to turn that let down in life into a burpee. That is Redemption:

13 Fatherhood
-*The State of being a father.*

Fathering isn't something that perfect men do , but something that perfects the man

Frank Pittman

What does this mean to you?
What is a Dad, a Father to you?

Well to me a Father in my eyes is a Provider, A Father is a Leader, A Father is a Super Hero in his own right. Someone more than capable at times in making the impossible, actually possible. A man that's willing in everyone to sacrifice himself for the family he brought into this world and the woman he loves. A Father isn't a part time title, it's a fulltime , 24 hour job.

So now ask yourself, Are you ready for Fatherhood?
Chances are you're looking at yourself right now and saying "Hell no"!. An you are absolutely right , but what if you were forced into the situation, would you be willing to step up to the plate and hit a homerun. By becoming everything that child and the woman giving birth to her needs. In today's world, too many young men are growing up in fatherless homes and not learning naturally all of these characteristics we've been talking about in and throughout this book. Young men are running from responsibility at a rapid pace and young men, born with so much potential in this world. They are being brought up with no principals, no morals, no respect for elders and so many other terrible things.

I remember vividly times sitting on the porch hoping my dad would show up when he said he'd pick me up. I remember days where I called a beeper number , never to get a answer back ,after all of the countless voicemails I'd send. I remember the football, Basketball, Baseball games where I would look into the stands and not see myself in anyone in the stands. That self being my creator, my dad himself, watching me and cheering me on.

Fatherhood is a serious responsibility and choosing the right woman, as well as being the right man for the woman your choosing to indulge with. Its all one huge responsibility and something you shouldn't do until your absolutely positively ready. In this lifetime alone, I've unfortunately had t00 many Abortions done. All of which still hurt me till this day, child is a blessing and I feel like on three occasions I missed out on that blessing.

My first one came, a few weeks into the school year, my Senior year, my girlfriend I had been dating since the previous school year and summer. She had come to school and brought to my attention that she had been 3 months pregnant. When I was presented the news I was devastated. My god mom who supported me always told me that If I went and had a child or been arrested. She would cut me off completely. No questions asked! I was always good to this girl so she thought I wanted this kid and was ready to take on the responsibility. An I totally wasn't but when I look back at that experience. In so many ways I was a coward, I'll never know what my life would be like if I had that child. How that child could've been my blessing, kept me from making so many mistakes. I often think about how it would've changed me , cause I knew I grew up without my dad. I would've wanted to give that kid all of the time and attention I never received. Having that child I know would've kept me from doing so many immature things at the time.

I often analyze the relationship I have with that God mom and the fear of being cut off by her. I now can honestly say wasn't worth it, my gf at the time went on to get the abortion and I went on to play football and eventually set off to college.

My second Mishap came a few years later while in College, My ex was pregnant by me but didn't tell me and got the abortion without my knowledge. When she told me the news I was so hurt because she made a decision to not have it without me . In this lifetime young men one of two things can happen. She can get rid of it without your knowledge, or she can keep it as well and not tell you until it's too late. But what you have to ask yourself is if all of sudden I got the late text or phone call. Will you be ready to step up to the plate? This time I was certain I would've, I wouldn't have been a coward. I didn't get the opportunity to unfortunately.

My third abortion occurred with a woman I thought I would be with forever. I can teach you a lesson now, Falling head over heels with someone without truly getting to know them will always hurt you in the long run . Because along the way you will continuously notice and learn things about them that you may or may not find appealing. This girl on the other hand, I thought had the same mindset I did but she totally didn't.

So there's this thing young men , in which women do to men , to get what they want out of them. That thing is called Trapped, yes women will purposely get pregnant by you in order to fulfil there selfish needs. My ex had her own motives for dating me and when I caught on , I had to make a selfish decision. I didn't want her to abort but her actions throughout the early pregnancy proved to me that she wasn't the women for me. Her actions proved to me that this isn't a woman I want to have and build a family with in the long run. I had to have a talk I never thought Id be having again. I respectfully asked that she get rid of the child.

I knew that kid would've suffered. I couldn't work up the courage to raise a beautiful child in a broken home. So I didn't, and that beautiful love story went sour really fast. Shortly after, she was on to the next man.

My last mishap came at the age of 27, with a girl I thought legit was the one . I honestly felt it in my heart that this was the one. But you notice as you get older, you can't mold someone into the person you want them to be. When you love someone , you have to love them for their flaws and all. Everything they are today, is just what they'll be, nothing more, nothing less. I found out while on vacation that I was expected to be a dad. We were overjoyed, told our families, and friends. I thought it was all perfect timing. Then it happened, she told me she actually didn't want to have the child . I was devastated because I felt as though Karma hit me , and hit me very hard. Here I am wanting this child a 100% . An here is my gf telling me 5 weeks pregnant that she isn't on the same page. When she got the abortion I felt so much anger towards her because I was already more than willing to start a family and give my all to my families happiness. It made me feel extremely worthless.

An I share these stories with you as embarrassing as they may be , to show you that although you escape the bullet, It can still be damaging. Now even attempt to imagine my life if I had these 4 kids , in all four instances. Having fun partying with friends whenever I want would be out the door, and very limited. Going to trips whenever I want, whenever I want wouldn't be possible. I would be living for something bigger than me. But for the young men put in this position, put your big boy pants on. Your living for more than you, Sacrifice because a key word in your life and forevermore. Ask any many doing the job of "Fatherhood" there's no greater joy than being responsible for someone else's happiness and actually making them happy.

So to make things simple. If you're going to mess with women out of wedlock, if you're going to be a player and play the game. Be safe and don't create responsibilities you aren't ready for. Because the worst thing you can do is bring someone into this world without your presence. Young men and Women , need someone to look up to, honor and respect that's going to set a bar in their lives for them to reach.

Be a teen when you're a teenage, a young adult when that time comes . An a father when you know you're ready!

I fortunately had great example of real men in my life, from my two best friends dads , Julio and David, to my cousins Raymond Graham and Uncle Hak. To mentors in the community , my mentor and big brother Mr. Cruz. I'm thankful for the example of what real men and being a father and provider are. I'm thankful for all the examples I've noticed in an throughout my community from Pop Warner Coaches, to men in the community that have taken the time to give me small peps talks here and there. The examples are there you just have to pay attention to them.

14 Individuality

-The quality of character of a person or thing that distinguishes them from others of the same kind , especially when strongly marked.

Be who you are and say what you feel, because those who mind don't matter , and those that matter don't mind

Bernard M. Baruch

Define Stereotype

What's the typical stereotype for your ethnicity or color?

What makes you different?

Being a African American Male from the inner city, the stereotype I'm labeled with is being someone who loves chicken and hip-hop, hanging in the streets and ultimately living to become nothing. Then statistics showed that although I didn't want to be dead or in Jail by the age of twenty one. Like the great Jay Z once said, Men lie, Women lie but numbers don't. And that stat was proven by the endless friends and family I've lost to the streets throughout my life. As well as the numerous friends and family I know that are currently in and out of Jail.

Something always told me in my heart I was different from what the stats or any stereotypes labeled me. Growing up although I was African American, I grew up in Puerto Rican Households. My best friend Julio would bring me to his family parties ever so often and there is where I was first introduce to the Spanish culture. Where it was the amazing, delicious Paste Lon his mom would make everyone once in a while because it took so long to cook, To the Empanadas she would be bowls full and we would all eat about 3 to 4 each. All the way to the deserts, the Upside down cake. Going to that house each day I noticed now. How much those experiences each day changed me from the typical kids that I knew grew up in my neighborhood. Their family would go camping which introduced me to the outdoors, Beaches where although I knew I was too dark. I was introduced to tanning. My horizons were fully expanded . I would honestly say I knew more as a teenage than some of the "men" I knew in my neighborhood. These experiences molded me, I didn't just like Chicken, because I knew that there were more , delicious foods out there. You know had to know what they were and ultimately how to make them.

In middle school I met my other best friend DJ and his family was the party family, Whether it was a cookout, or family gathering. His beautiful grandma Marina would always dance , and in her household whenever all the family would meet up they would listen to music. The music they listened to was totally different from the music I often heard. It was in a different language but something about it I felt like made my soul dance. After months had past , one family gathering I was brave enough to step on the dance floor. DJ's cousin macho was like our older brother and he called me out to dance with his cousin my age. On that dance floor is where I learned how to dance Bachata, eventually I learned Merengue and still till this dance. I don't know what I'm doing when salsa comes on but it just feels right to move to it.

So let's slow down a bit, I'm black, I live in the hood, but if you got to know me you would know that I love Spanish food and Spanish music. These things made me an individual. These interest being where I was from made me different. In my neighborhood , men would be seen wearing saggy jeans, wave caps on their heads, timbs or Nikes or the latest Jordan's. I for one can admit at a point I fell victim to following trends. But I knew in my heart the things I was wearing weren't me. They didn't say Jalil, this kid that's adventurous ,black but loves Spanish music.

During my freshman year of high school my older brother had obtained his first job. Growing up I thought he was the coolest person ever because of the things he was always in. From the Video games he played, to the friends he had. They were all , always so different from everyone else but would often be talked about. Called nerds etc. but no one bullied my brother because he could revert and get just as angry or aggressive as the toughest dude in the neighborhood. I remember when one day my brother came home from shopping, Him and his best friend mark would come home with bags of cloths and show off the outfits they had gotten. I noticed a brand called "American Eagle". It was very popular in my neighborhood because everything everyone was wearing was baggy. Long white t shirts etc., these clothes on the other hand were fitted to your body. To wear them you had to have the right size that fit your body. It was a clean look that you only saw in suburban neighborhoods. I noticed how perfectly fit the jacket was to my brothers body, the jeans that were fitted just person not too baggy , not too loose. To top things off the shoes he chose to wear as well. A brand called "Lacoste" I didn't know what that was but I knew if I had the money I wouldn't mind wearing the same exact things. My brother knew he was on to something but he wasn't ready for the judgement that came with it.

When you decide to do something different from everyone else, your often labeled an outcast and that's what people did to my older brother. They didn't understand him and what was wearing so the first thing they did was judge him. My brother was a pretty boy at a time where being a gangster and gangster rap was highly promoted. Gangsters didn't wear fitted clothes and if your clothes were fitted. A lot of people considered you to be gay, corny, a weirdo.

My brother eventually folded to this judgement and reverted back like he had something to prove to people. It eventually led to him , getting wrapped up into a bunch of trouble and ending up ultimately in jail because he felt like he tried to be different and failed. But in my eyes he didn't because he planted a seed In me. See I noticed all people have their own perceptions , opinions of things. But when you do what you want, or feel, that is what is ultimately right. Life isn't about doing what everyone else is doing, It's about being you and living your life the way you want to. My brother planted a seed in me, but I was more prepared for the stones that would be thrown at me.

As I grew older I noticed at dances in high school , when Spanish music would come on all black men would sit down. An I'd see only the Spanish guys who weren't shy dancing with all of the girls. In what people feared, I saw opportunity, I learned Spanish music was all in the hips and when you dance bachata music it was ,1,2,3 jump change direction and do it again. I learned Merengue was just a hip side to side movement. I took these small lessons and jumped on the dance floor. An too my surprise, although my black friends would have nothing but jokes for me. My Spanish friends were actually impressed, After years of doing it, I eventually became the black guy to my friends that loved Spanish music. It made me happy so I listened and danced to it. Not just in parties but on my own time as well. It opened doors for me , friends , relationships.

I share these stories with you because it's what being a individual is about, it's about doing what makes you happy. Don't be subjected to your color or ethnicities norms. Be different, explore, try new things because you never know what you may truly love someday and what experience could change your life.

Thank you

This book has been all of me, my values, my beliefs the people I respect and love and I've shared their stories with you as well. Hopefully this book has taught you something. Brought awareness about things that you didn't understand before reading. This book to me was me opening my heart to you and letting you know that success isn't a straight line and it is about falling down to get back up stronger than ever. But I've come to the conclusion that everyone doesn't have to fall. If we smarten up and take the time to learn from others mistakes. I don't want you to be just as good as me, I want you to be better. I was heard a speech in which Mrs. Farrakhan said a great leader doesn't not lead people to himself, but steps to the side and leads them to something far much greater than 'Himself'. I don't want you to be the best Jalil or any of my mentors, friends. I want you to be greater than all of them. Be the best you that you can be and happiness will enter your life. There are things you may or may not agree with but I want you to make this book your book! Thank you for reading.

Jalil Q. Oates

Made in the USA
Middletown, DE
03 August 2018